AMERICAN INDIAN ART AND CULTURE

The Navajo

RENNAY CRAATS

PRINCIPAL PHOTOGRAPHY BY MARILYN "ANGEL" WYNN

CHELSEA CLUBHOUSE

An Imprint of Chelsea House Publishers

A Haights Cross Communications Company

Philadelphia

This edition first published in 2004 in the United States of America by Chelsea Clubhouse, a division of Chelsea House Publishers and a subsidiary of Haights Cross Communications.

Chelsea Clubhouse
1974 Sproul Road, Suite 400
Broomall, PA 19008-0914

The Chelsea House world wide web address is www.chelseahouse.com

Library of Congress Cataloging-in-Publication Data

Craats, Rennay.
  The Navajo / Rennay Craats.
     v. cm. -- (American Indian art and culture)
Includes bibliographical references and index.
Contents: The people -- Navajo homes -- Navajo communities -- Navajo
clothing -- Navajo food -- Tools and technology -- Navajo religion --
Ceremonies and celebrations -- Music and dance -- Language and
storytelling -- Navajo art -- Special feature -- Studying the Navajos'
past.
  ISBN 0-7910-7961-9 (Chelsea House) (lib. bdg. : alk. paper)
  1. Navajo Indians--History--Juvenile literature. 2. Navajo
Indians--Social life and customs--Juvenile literature. [1. Navajo
Indians.] I. Title. II. Series.
  E99.N3C789 2004
  978.9004'9726--dc22

                             2003017529
                    Printed in the United States of America
                    1 2 3 4 5 6 7 8 9 0 07 06 05 04 03

©2004 WEIGL EDUCATIONAL PUBLISHERS LIMITED

Project Coordinator   Heather C. Hudak   **Copy Editor**   Jennifer Nault   **Design**   Janine Vangool   **Layout**   Terry Paulhus   **Photo Researcher**   Wendy Cosh   **Chelsea Clubhouse Editors**   Sally Cheney and Margaret Brierton   **Validator**   Eugene B. Joe "Baatsoslanii"

Cover: Monument Valley (Marilyn "Angel" Wynn), Navajo Woman (Marilyn "Angel" Wynn, Navajo Baskets (Marilyn "Angel" Wynn, Navajo Rock Art (Marilyn "Angel" Wynn); Kit Breen: pages 9, 17, 22, 30; Courtesy LeRoy DeJolie: page 27; Ann Purcell: page 15; Cheryl Richter: pages 5, 11B, 16; Marilyn "Angel" Wynn: pages 1, 3, 6, 7, 8, 10, 11T, 12, 13, 14, 18, 19, 20, 21, 23, 24, 25T, 25B, 26, 28T, 28B, 29, 31.

Please note
At the time of printing, the Internet addresses appearing in this book were correct. Owing to the dynamic nature of the Internet, however, we cannot guarantee that all these addresses will remain correct.

CONTENTS

The People

It is difficult to imagine that a group of people lived in the United States nearly 1,000 years ago. The Navajo first settled in the southwestern United States between 1200 and 1500. Today, the Navajo is one of the largest American Indian tribes in the United States. More than sixty **clans** live in Arizona, Colorado, New Mexico, and Utah.

The Navajo traveled from Canada to the United States between the 13th and 16th centuries. They moved from place to place around the Southwest, hunting animals and gathering food. They also raided **Pueblo** farming settlements. The Navajo first encountered the Spanish and the Mexicans in the 17th century. The Navajo received horses, goats, and sheep from the Spanish. The Mexicans taught the Navajo silversmithing. The Pueblo shared their weaving and pottery-making techniques. These skills changed the Navajo's ways of life, and became very important to their economy. Over time, the Navajo became shepherds and farmers, too.

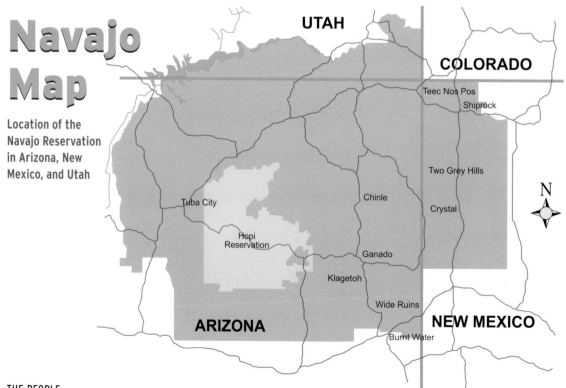

Navajo Map

Location of the Navajo Reservation in Arizona, New Mexico, and Utah

UTAH

COLORADO

Teec Nos Pos

Shiprock

Two Grey Hills

Tuba City

Chinle

Crystal

Hopi Reservation

Ganado

Klagetoh

Wide Ruins

ARIZONA

NEW MEXICO

Burnt Water

N

By the late 1800s, conflict erupted between the United States government and the Navajo. In 1863, U.S. forces destroyed Navajo homes and crops, and took their livestock. Thousands of Navajo were captured or forced to surrender to U.S. troops. The captives were forced to walk to a reservation at Fort Sumner, New Mexico. Their **deportation** is known as the "Long Walk." Many people died along the 300-mile (483-kilometers) trek. Even after they arrived at Fort Sumner, many Navajo continued to suffer. Some died of disease. Others died of starvation due to crop failures, and more died in conflicts with Apache prisoners who were also being held captive by the U.S. government. In 1868, a treaty was signed, which allowed the surviving Navajo to return to their territory where a new reservation had been built.

Since then, the Navajo Nation has grown. The Navajo try to find ways to balance modern culture with their traditional ways. Today, many Navajo work in cities in careers such as medicine, education, and law. However, they still recognize their elders' beliefs.

Today, about 270,000 Navajo live in the United States. Some Navajo live in cities. Others live on reservation land that covers more than 16 million acres (6,474,970 hectares). The tribe took its name from the Pueblo word *Navahu*, meaning "planters of huge fields." The Navajo call themselves *Dineh* or *Diné*. This means "The People" in the Navajo language.

Navajo people young and old enjoy attending the Navajo Nation Fair, held every September. More then 100,000 people attend the 5-day gala.

Navajo Homes

The first Navajo who arrived in the United States did not need permanent houses. They were **nomadic**. The Navajo did not stay in one place for very long. They moved to areas where there were many animals to hunt. When they learned to farm and raise livestock, the Navajo built permanent communities. They built homes called **hogans**. Each hogan housed an extended Navajo family. The first **fork-stick** hogans were cone-shaped homes that had five sides. The Navajo covered hogans with mud and bark to protect them from the weather. In areas where winters were cold, clay or mud walls were made thicker for extra protection. Hearth fires heated hogans. A hole at the top of the hogan allowed smoke from the fires to escape.

Although most Navajo peoples no longer live in hogans, they retain one for ceremonies.

DWELLING AND DECORATION

A short, covered passage attached to the eastern side of the hogan served as the building's entrance. The doorway was located on the eastern side of the structure so it would always face the rising Sun.

The Navajo carefully considered where to build each hogan. They would not build on gravesites, old battlegrounds, or areas where trees had been struck by lightning.

The kitchen in a Navajo hogan often contains utensils and spices for preparing food.

The introduction of the railroad in the early 1900s made large supplies of building materials, such as wooden crossties, available to the Navajo. This allowed the Navajo to construct larger, taller hogans, which had 6 or 8 sides. These structures were often made from stone and hardened clay brick called **adobe**. Today, hogans have one round room that is about 23 feet (7 meters) across. These large buildings are most often used for ceremonies and **curings**. Ceremonial hogans can be as large as 50 feet (15.2 meters) wide. These structures are the center of the Navajo's spiritual lives. In some areas, the Navajo still live in hogans.

Navajo Communities

The first Navajo were hunter-gatherers. They hunted deer and small game and gathered wild plants for food. The Navajo learned another way of life when they met the Pueblo peoples. The Pueblo taught the Navajo how to plant crops. In the 1600s, the Navajo also adopted the Pueblo peoples practice of raising livestock. Sheep became very important to the Navajo's survival. Sheep provided meat for food as well as wool to make blankets and clothing. The Navajo often stole sheep and horses from Spanish settlers. The Navajo also traveled to neighboring communities where they would trade handmade goods for canned foods, tools, and other manufactured items. The Navajo produced well-known goods, such as baskets, blankets, and rugs. Some settlers visited the Navajo reservation's trading posts to buy these handmade crafts.

Over time, life for the Navajo has changed. Many Navajo have left reservation land to

Navajo families spend time together celebrating their past. Some families, like the one pictured here, hike the Apache Trail of Tears.

live and work in surrounding cities. The discovery of oil and other minerals, such as uranium, on reservation land has boosted the Navajo Nation's economy. The Navajo Nation Council was established to govern these resources as well as life on the reservation. This council is the largest American-Indian government in the United States. With an elected tribal president, vice-president, and 88 council delegates, this complex government body creates laws and decides on punishments for individuals who break these laws.

The Navajo are the largest American-Indian group in the country. More than 165,000 Navajo live on reservation land. This land is called the Navajo Nation. The Navajo Nation is larger than West Virginia.

Today, many Navajo live in modern houses rather than traditional-style hogans. They also continue to make traditional crafts and art. The Navajo are still well known for their detailed pottery, blankets, and silver jewelry. Techniques for making these items have been passed on from earlier generations.

Many Navajo continue to practice the traditions of their **ancestors**. For example, many still speak the Navajo language. Another tradition the Navajo maintain is to marry outside their clans. Although clan members are not always blood relatives, they consider themselves "related" because they share the same clan.

In 1923, the Navajo Nation established a tribal government. Today, the Navajo Nation Council is the largest American Indian government in the United States.

Navajo Clothing

Many Navajo honor their culture by wearing traditional clothing. Both men and women wear moccasins. These hard-soled boots can be worn short or knee-high. They are often decorated with colorful beads or detailed **embroidery**. Moccasins are made in a variety of colors and with such materials as buckskin, leather, and suede. The top of the moccasins are often folded over. The Navajo were known to carry knives and other small items in these folds.

Even today, many Navajo wear traditional clothing. Others prefer to wear traditional clothing only for special events, such as this parade.

Traditionally, Navajo women wore basic skirts made from antelope, deer, or buffalo skins. They made dresses by sewing together woven blankets. They added beads or fringe to decorate the clothing. Women eventually began trading deerskins and weaving wool for cotton shawls and other European clothes. Over time, Navajo styles were replaced with American- and European-inspired clothing, such as long, pleated velvet, wool, or cotton skirts. Women also began wearing long-sleeved blouses that matched the skirts.

Traditionally, Navajo men wore ankle-length, leather leggings and buckskin loincloths. During the winter months, men wore long-sleeved buckskin shirts. The men were also influenced by other cultures. The neighboring Pueblo peoples introduced the Navajo to long pants. Many Navajo men began wearing Mexican-inspired styles. For example, they wore blankets over one shoulder and mid-calf pants that had silver buttons down each side.

Early Navajo wore blankets as protection from cold weather.

ADORNMENTS

The Navajo word for a squash blossom necklace means "bead that spreads out."

Today, many Navajo combine traditional clothing with modern fashions. While many Navajo men wear blue jeans and cowboy boots, some wear Navajo **turquoise** jewelry. The Navajo still add detailed embroidery and beadwork to their clothing. Men, women, and children also wear traditional clothing for ceremonies and special occasions. The Navajo also combine traditional ways of wearing their hair with modern styles. For example, some wear their hair in a traditional bun. Others wear their hair loose or they wear it in braids for powwows or ceremonies.

Navajo Food

Once the Navajo became farmers and shepherds, their diet changed. They no longer needed to hunt game and gather plants. Instead, they ate the animals they raised and the crops they harvested. **Mutton** and goat were valuable food sources. They also ate beans, corn, and squash. Corn was an important staple for many American Indian peoples.

The Navajo use food to welcome visitors and express thanks.

Navajo diets did not include many dairy products. Many Navajo were **lactose-intolerant**. People who are lactose-intolerant cannot digest lactose, a sugar found in milk. Milk is an important source of calcium, which is a mineral that keeps bones strong. Instead of milk, the Navajo ate juniper ash to keep their bones strong. Juniper ash contains a great deal of calcium. To create juniper ash, the Navajo burned juniper branches and ground the ashes into a powder. The Navajo added the powder to traditional breads and blue cornmeal dishes.

For the Navajo, food has special meaning. It is used to welcome guests, and it is a way to give thanks for their belongings.

Traditional Navajo recipes are passed down from mother to daughter. Many Navajo recipes have never been recorded. The Navajo have always cooked from memory, using their fingers and hands to measure ingredients. The Navajo did not have ovens. Instead, traditional cooks prepared meals over an open fire.

Navajo cooks use plants and vegetables, such as cactus, cedar brush, and onions, to make dishes unique. For example, cedar brush is still used to add color and flavor to blue cornmeal pudding. Another Navajo food is fry bread. Use the following recipe to make this traditional snack.

Ingredients:
2 cups (473.2 ml) flour
1 tbsp. (14.8 ml) baking powder
1 tsp. (4.9 ml) salt
1 tbsp. (14.8 ml) vegetable oil
3/4 cup (177.4 ml) warm water
oil for frying
powdered sugar, honey, or honey butter

Equipment:
large bowl
plastic bag
wooden spoon
rolling pin
wok or deep skillet
tongs or slotted spatula
paper towel

Navajo Fry Bread

1. Mix dry ingredients together. Stir in oil and water. Mix until smooth.

2. Knead lightly for 1 minute. Do not work the dough too much or it will not become flat.

3. Shape the dough into a ball. Put the dough ball in a plastic bag and refrigerate for 1 hour.

4. Remove the dough ball from the refrigerator. Pinch off 12 small balls of dough and flatten each into 3- or 4-inch (7.6- or 10-centimeter) circles. Roll each circle. The thinner the dough circles, the better they will puff in the oil.

5. Poke a hole in the center of each circle with your finger.

6. Lightly dust the tops of the circles with flour while the oil heats in a wok or deep skillet to 375° F (190° C). One at a time, place the circles into the hot oil and brown for about 1 minute on each side. Use the tongs or slotted spatula to turn the circles.

7. Dry each circle on paper towels.

8. Top each circle with powdered sugar, honey, honey butter, or your favorite topping, and enjoy.

Tools, Weapons, and Defense

Tools helped to make life easier for the Navajo. Many tools, such as ladles, spoons, and dishes, were used every day. These tools were often made from dried gourds or carved from wood.

The Navajo used tools to harvest and prepare corn. They dried corn in order to preserve it for use throughout the year. First, corn was placed in a pot of water over hot coals overnight. Then in the morning, the corn kernels were scraped from the cob and placed in the Sun to dry. Finally, the Navajo used two pieces of stone to grind the dried kernels into cornmeal. A *mano*, or tube-like stone, was rubbed against a flat stone called the *metate* to grind the kernels.

The Navajo used large looms to weave. According to legend, Spider Woman taught Navajo women to weave. Spider Man gave her directions to build a loom.

WEAVING LOOMS AND HUNTING ARROWS

The Navajo were well known for their woven rugs, which also required special tools. To make rugs, the Navajo used upright **looms** and **spindlewhorls** to twist threads together. This created stronger fibers for weaving. Other weaving tools included rods and sticks that were used to separate threads and weave designs into fabric.

The Navajo used tools to make silver jewelry, too. First, they carved designs into a soft rock. They used the carved rock as a mold to **cast** silver. Navajo jewelers used awls to punch designs into the silver pieces. Later, fine files and other tools allowed Navajo silversmiths to make more refined markings on even smaller pieces of metal.

Navajo Indians use many tools to make jewelry.

The bow and arrow was an important weapon for Navajo warriors. The Navajo did not have access to quality hardwood so their bows were shorter than those made by other American Indian groups. They made arrows from plant shoots and ram horns. The horns were drilled, sanded, and polished to form arrow shafts. The Navajo also collected arrowheads from abandoned **pueblo** villages. They could also make arrows from flint. The bow and arrow was a useful hunting tool, which helped make the Navajo a successful tribe.

Navajo Religion

Religion is an important part of the Navajo's life. All occasions, from daily life to seasonal responsibilities, are celebrated. For example, rituals are performed to ask the spirits for help during a hunt. The Navajo also bless hogans when they are built.

The Navajo religion is based on a number of gods who are associated with items found in nature. These gods influence the happenings in the Navajo Nation. The Navajo believe in good and evil ghosts. They believe that in order to have peace and harmony in the world, there must be a strong connection between Earth's different elements. They honor spirits through ceremonies and daily prayer in order to keep this balance.

Window Rock is a sacred Navajo site. The town of Window Rock is the capital of the Navajo Nation.

Medicine men and women remain an important part of Navajo religion. They are still powerful members of the community. They use chants, prayers, and songs to help heal people. Sometimes, they prescribe herbs to help the sick. Other times, **prayer bundles** are prescribed to cure a specific problem. A medicine person can also be a "headman."

The Native American Church (NAC) is an American Indian religion that is popular among some Navajo peoples. The religion is based on drinking or eating the peyote cactus bud. According to this religion, the peyote holds the heart, soul, and memory of the Creator. Eating peyote is thought to bring the individual and the Creator together.

Navajo religion includes several sacred places where the religion must be practiced. Four mountains–Blanca Peak in Colorado, Mount Taylor in New Mexico, the San Francisco Peaks in Arizona, and Hesperus Peak in Colorado–are sacred to the Navajo. They believe the Creator placed Navajo people between these four posts, and they should never leave this holy homeland.

Monument Valley is another sacred Navajo site. Monument Valley is located in the Navajo Nation and is one of the most photographed places on Earth.

Ceremonies and Celebrations

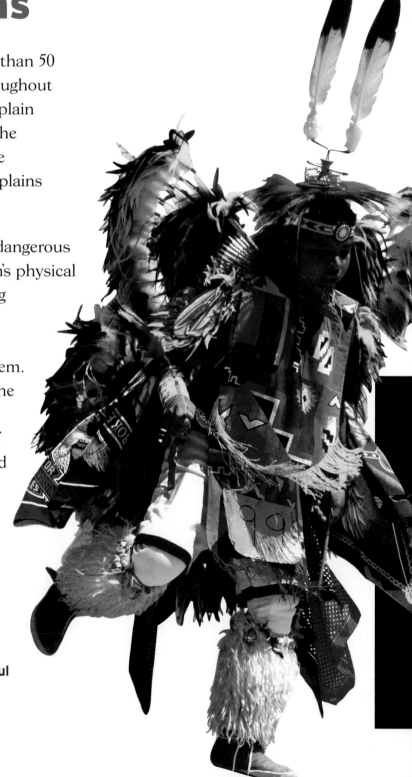

The Navajo perform more than 50 different ceremonies throughout the year. Some ceremonies explain events that occur in nature. The *Keshjee'*, or Shoe Game, is one such sacred ceremony that explains the origins of day and night.

A healing ceremony controls dangerous powers and balances a person's physical and spiritual self. Each healing ceremony is different. Chants and rituals are chosen based on the patient's specific problem. Patients draw strength from the wisdom of medicine men and women as well as a mixture of herbs. The tribe may also hold healing sings to help cure sickness. Chants or songs, herbs, and sandpaintings are combined to help a person become well again.

Dancing is an important part of some ceremonies. The Fancy Dance uses colorful costumes and quick and spinning footwork.

Healing ceremonies can last more than one week. Each day of the ceremony, a different song or chant is performed to help cure the patient.

The Navajo perform ceremonies as part of their daily lives, too. New buildings are blessed with prayers. Sometimes songs, dances, costumes, and sandpaintings are included as part of these ceremonies. The Navajo House Blessing Ceremony is called *hooghan da ashdlisigil*. This event brings balance, harmony, good luck, and well-being to the people living in the house. The Navajo believe the ceremony will also block bad dreams, evil spirits, hardship, and sickness from entering the house.

MYTHOLOGY

Some ceremonies celebrate events and figures in Navajo mythology. For example, the Blessingway Ceremony is a two-day ceremony that celebrates the story of Changing Woman, a main figure in Navajo religion. Changing Woman was the child of First Man and First Woman. Changing Woman rubbed skin off her body to create the four original Navajo clans. These clans are the ancestors of all Navajo peoples. The Navajo believe the Blessingway Ceremony brings peace, harmony, safety, and long, happy lives to their people. The ceremony is often performed to celebrate marriages, protect warriors from enemies, and to help women during childbirth.

The Fire Dance is so named because it takes place around a ceremonial fire. It is sometimes called the Corral Dance because it is usually held in a brush corral.

Music and Dance

Music is a powerful part of the Navajo culture. It is an important part of special ceremonies, as well as daily events. Song lyrics tell stories about Navajo history and life. These songs are passed down orally, so the narrative, or story, is repeated many times. This makes it easier to learn and remember the song. Usually, the Nation's chief leads the singing. Songs are believed to possess healing powers, and many Navajo sing to bring about a desired event.

Most Navajo music is in the form of chants that are performed during ceremonies. Bells, drumbeats, and rattles keep detailed rhythms in time. Ceremonial singing is intended to cure illness. The length of a healing chant varies, depending on the illness it is designed for. Since some ceremonies can last for several days, a chant can include more than 500 songs and thousands of lines.

Navajo children start dancing at a very young age. There are dancing events at powwows for children.

CEREMONIAL DANCING

The Navajo perform the *Yeibichai* songs during the Nightway Ceremony. This ceremony takes place at the end of a 9-night ritual. The Nightway Ceremony calls upon the *Yeis*, a group of Holy People, to help the Navajo restore harmony. During the ceremony, a team of 14 dancers—the leader Yeibachai, or Talking God, six men, six women, and the Water Sprinkler—perform the Yeibachai Dance before dawn. They sing the "Bluebird Song" at the end of the ceremony. The bluebird represents happiness and peace. Dancers wear blue, brown, or gray masks, and attach fox pelts to their belts. The Talking God dancer wears a white mask with 12 eagle feathers. The dancers remove their masks during the event to show children that they are not **supernatural** beings.

Many Navajo ceremonies feature traditional dancing. Dancers' costumes and masks represent spirits, gods, and animals. Often, dancers act out stories and myths using colorful hoops and traditional clothing. One important ritual is the Fire Dance, or Mountainway Dance. Participants lunge at each other with firebrands as they dance.

Gourd rattles are popular music-makers for the Navajo.

Language and Storytelling

The Navajo language is part of the Athapaskan language family. The Athapaskan language was developed in northwestern Canada and is related to the languages spoken by the Hupa and the Apache peoples. The Navajo language is complicated and it is very different from English. One Navajo word can have many meanings. A slight change in the **pronunciation** of a word changes its meaning. The Navajo language contains many unusual sounds. The Navajo sounds "tt'," "t'," "ts'," "k'," and "ch'" cannot be translated into English. This makes it difficult for people of other cultures to learn and remember the Navajo language.

The Navajo celebrate the first time a Navajo child laughs out loud. This celebration is called the First Laugh rite.

For hundreds of years, the Navajo language was only spoken. The Navajo did not have a written language until the early 1900s. When **linguists** began recording the Navajo language, they wrote the words exactly as they sounded when they were spoken. Today, the Navajo have both a written and spoken language. Still, many of their stories are passed from generation to generation orally.

Storytellers pass on the Navajo culture and tradition to younger generations. Storytellers entertain listeners and teach them how to live according to tradition. Navajo stories explain the history of the Navajo and how they have **evolved**. Many stories share common themes and patterns. One common pattern is the use of the number four. Four represents the seasons, the directions, and the sacred mountains surrounding the Navajo homeland. The number four is also present in tales about mythological figures, such as Spider Woman, Monster Slayer, Changing Woman, and the Sun. These stories have been told for centuries.

Laughter and humor are an important part of the Navajo language. The First Laugh rite is one example of how humor and laughter are celebrated in the Navajo culture. The first time a Navajo baby laughs aloud is considered cause for a celebration and feast. The person who made the child laugh is honored during the celebration.

Rock art is an example of how traditional Navajo stories are told using pictures.

Navajo Art

Very skilled Navajo artists create detailed, handmade arts and crafts. Navajo blankets, rugs, and jewelry are well known throughout the United States. Most Navajo arts and crafts are linked to their traditions and religion.

The Navajo use silver and turquoise to make bracelets, necklaces, earrings, belt buckles, and rings. Navajo artists learned silversmithing from Mexican and Spanish settlers in the 19th century. These artists melted down United States' silver dollar coins and Mexican pesos to create silver pieces. Navajo artists soon added turquoise to simple ornaments and buttons.

Spaniards and Mexicans introduced the Navajo to the art of silversmithing.

Navajo women have been expert weavers since the 1600s. Navajo women learned to weave from the Pueblo peoples. The Navajo used sheep's wool to create rugs and blankets. European traders asked Navajo women to weave rugs and blankets in specific designs using pre-spun, colored yarn. The traders returned to their homelands and sold these pieces. Today, weavers mix creative patterns with traditional designs and techniques. Patterns and colors are named according to where they are made, such as Wide Ruins, Two Gray Hills, and Chinle.

Navajo baskets are usually woven from **sumac**. Navajo weavers begin a basket by making a coil or knot. Then they wind the sumac around the outer edge of the coil or knot. Baskets are very important to the Navajo. They represent the basket owner's well-being. Ceremonial baskets are called *Ts'aa'*. Ts'aa' are used to hold objects such as prayersticks or medicine bundles during rituals. They hold food during a wedding ceremony or ground clay, red ochre, and cornmeal during the *kinaalda'*, a coming of age ceremony. Baskets can be used as drums, too.

The basket represents the well-being of an individual.

DRY ART

Sandpainting, or dry painting, is an art form and a ceremonial practice. Ceremonies, sacred songs, and spiritual figures are pictured in sandpaintings. These pieces of art are most often used during healing ceremonies. Medicine men and women create sandpaintings to help treat patients. They use colored sands and finely ground charcoal, cornmeal, pollen, and colored rocks to create an appropriate image on the floor of the hogan. The patient sits on the completed painting. The Navajo believe sandpaintings absorb evil spirits. The evil spirits will harm the Navajo if the painting is not destroyed. The painting is created and destroyed between sunrise and sunset.

Navajo Code Talkers

During World War II, the **Allies** used the Navajo language to create a code that the Japanese army could not understand.

In 1942, Navajo marine recruits began working on codes. Navajo marines created a dictionary of military words and terms. They could **encode**, send, and **decode** a three-line message in 20 seconds. Before the Navajo code, machines took 30 minutes to encode and then decode the same text.

A code talker translated a collection of unrelated Navajo words into English. Combining the first letters of each English word spelled out a message. For example, the Navajo word *wol-la-chee* means "ant." It represented the letter "A." About 450 common military words were also translated into Navajo code words. For example, the Navajo used *besh-lo*, which means "iron fish," to represent a submarine, and *dah-he-tih-hi*, which means "hummingbird," to refer to a fighter plane.

Code talkers served in all six U.S. Marine divisions. They were part of every assault in the Pacific Ocean between 1942 and 1945. About 375 to 420 Navajo soldiers served as code talkers during World War II.

MODERN ARTIST

LeRoy DeJolie

LeRoy DeJolie is a Navajo photographer. He lives in the small community of Lechee, Arizona. DeJolie has been taking photographs for more than twenty years. He is inspired by the landscapes and traditions of the Navajo Reservation, where he was raised. DeJolie has spent much time exploring and observing his surroundings. These observations help him capture the beauty of the Arizona landscape.

DeJolie uses different types of cameras to take photographs in various sizes. His specialty is large-format photography. Large format cameras use larger film. This allows the photographer to capture more detail and create larger images.

DeJolie was one of the photographers featured in the PBS television special _Images of Arizona._

DeJolie's landscape photographs show the stunning colors and textures of Arizona's canyons, rocks, and plains. DeJolie also photographs Navajo people. His photographs capture the vivid colors of traditional Navajo dress. For DeJolie, photography is a way of preserving Navajo memories and traditions for future generations.

DeJolie's photographs have been published around the world. He was the official photographer for the Navajo Nation's exhibit at the 2002 Olympic Games in Salt Lake City, Utah. His photographs have been shown in the Olympic Museum in Lausanne, Switzerland. DeJolie's work has been published in newspapers and magazines, including _Reader's Digest_, _The Washington Post_, _Native Peoples Magazine_, and _Arizona Highways_ magazine.

DeJolie is happy to share his knowledge with other photographers. In his workshops, he guides other photographers to his favorite places in northern Arizona. He teaches his students the techniques needed to capture the colors and textures of the land.

Studying the Navajo's Past

Many **anthropologists** and **archaeologists** believe the Navajo first **migrated** to Canada from Asia. They believe the Navajo traveled to the southwestern United States between 1400 and 1500—around the same time Spanish colonists arrived in the United States. However, oral histories told by Navajo storytellers suggest their people arrived near Chaco Canyon between 900 and 1130.

Tree-ring dating supports the Navajo's claim. In this method of dating artifacts and events, scientists study tree ring growth to determine when past events occurred or artifacts were made. This dating method suggests hogan-style homes found in Colorado date back to the 1100s. A homestead with Navajo features discovered south of Gallup, New Mexico, dated back to 1380. Many of these findings suggest the Navajo lived in the southwestern United States during the same period as the Pueblo peoples.

Scientists do not know exactly when the Navajo journeyed to their current home. Scientists need to collect more ancient artifacts to establish a definite time line. Many experts agree that the Navajo arrived between 800 and 1500.

The Navajo believed silver and turquoise were the most valuable forms of adornment. They wore jewelry as a symbol of beauty and wealth.

TIME LINE

Pre-10,000 – 6500 B.C.
Hunted animals and gathered plants.

1541
Francisco Vasquez de Coronado first meets the Navajo in New Mexico.

1583
Spanish colonists encounter the Navajo.

1600s
Conflict grows between Spanish and American Indian groups in New Mexico; many Navajo are kidnapped and forced into slavery.

The Navajo raid other American Indian villages and Spanish settlements.

1630 – 1680
The Navajo begin to herd sheep and horses.

1725 – 1740
The Navajo build pueblo villages.

1846
The Navajo and the United States government sign their first treaty.

1863
The U.S. government takes thousands of Navajo people captive. These people make the "Long Walk."

1864 – 1868
The Navajo and Apache are held captive in Bosque Redondo in Fort Sumner.

1868
A treaty establishes Navajo reservation land and a peace agreement between the Navajo and the U.S. government.

1923
The Navajo Nation Council is established.

1924
The Navajo become official U.S. citizens as part of the Citizenship Act.

1942
Navajo soldiers are recruited as code talkers.

The shape of a basket represents the Navajo's relationship with Mother Earth and Father Sky. Each shape has a different meaning.

Sandpainting

Sandpainting is a traditional Navajo activity. Sandpaintings used in healing ceremonies are rarely seen by other cultures. These sandpaintings are used to restore balance and make the patient well. The artist uses sand as well as crushed rock, crushed flowers, pollen, and gypsum to create these important images.

Ceremonial sandpaintings are not sold. Sandpaintings that are sold use sacred Navajo symbols, but in a way that respects the Navajo's cultural beliefs. Unlike ceremonial paintings, these pieces are created on flat pieces of wood. A glue base allows the artist to permanently place the sand, rock, and other ground materials in a pattern. This type of sandpainting allows other cultures to experience more of the Navajo culture.

You can make your own sandpainting.

STEP 1 Coat a piece of heavy cardboard with glue.

STEP 2 Then, sprinkle colored sand on the surface to make a picture.

Try to recreate a scene showing something that is important to you. This could include your family or a favorite hobby.

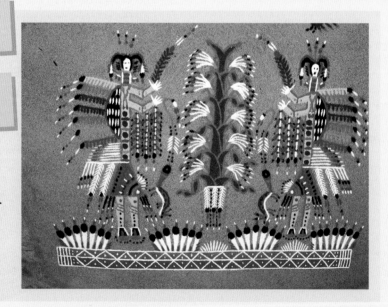

FURTHER READING

Further Reading

An accurate account of the history of the Navajo can be found in Susan Stan's book *The Navajo*, Rourke Publications, Inc., 1989. This book follows the Navajo story from prehistoric times to present day.

Another accurate source of information about the Navajo is Richard M. Gaines's book *The Navajo (Native Americans)*, Checkerboard Library, 2000. This book explores the Navajo history and community.

Web Sites

Learn more about Navajo code talkers at
www.usmint.gov/mint_programs/ medals/navajo

Learn more about the Navajo Nation at
www.navajo.org

Find out about the Navajo land, culture, and people at
www.americanwest.com/pages/navajo2.htm

GLOSSARY

adobe: sun-dried, clay brick

Allies: a group of countries that fought together during World War II

ancestors: family members from earlier generations

anthropologists: scientists who study human origins, development, customs, and beliefs

archaeologists: scientists who study objects from the past to learn about past civilizations

cast: to make something by pouring hot metal into a mold and allowing it to cool and harden

clans: groups of families that are related to each other

curings: healings

decode: to convert a message into a form that is understood

deportation: removing a person or people from a region or country

embroidery: decorating with needlework

encode: to convert a message into a code

evolved: developed

fork-stick: several logs placed in a tent-like formation

hogans: pyramid-shaped homes with five to eight sides

lactose-intolerant: unable to digest lactose, a sugar found in dairy products

linguists: people who study languages and their structure

looms: wooden frames used for weaving

migrated: moved from one place and settled in another place

mutton: meat from sheep

nomadic: people who move from place to place rather than settling in one area

prayer bundles: bundles of prayers that are prescribed to cure specific ailments

pronunciation: a way of speaking a word

Pueblo: a farming American Indian group who live in New Mexico and Arizona

pueblo: a flat-roofed, connected building made from dried mud

spindlewhorls: small wheels used to regulate the speed of spinning wheels

sumac: a shrub whose leaves are dried and ground for tanning and dyeing

supernatural: beyond the forces of nature; magical.

turquoise: greenish-blue gemstone

INDEX